YAS

LIFE IN THE MARINES

Robert C. Kennedy

Children's Press
A Division of Grolier Publishing
New York / London / Hong Kong / Sydney
Danbury, Connecticut

Book Design: Nelson Sa
Contributing Editor: Mark Beyer

Photo Credits: Cover © Corbis; p. 5 © Steve Raymer/Corbis; p. 7 © George Hall/Corbis; pp. 9, 11 © Corbis; p. 13 © Chris Rainier/Corbis; p. 15 © Robin Adshead; The Military Picture Library/Corbis; p. 16 © Bob Krist/Corbis; p. 19 © Danny Lehman/Corbis; p. 21 © Bob Krist/Corbis; pp. 22, 25 © Danny Lehman/Corbis; p. 26 © Leif Skoogfors/Corbis; p. 29 © Danny Lehman/Corbis; p. 31 © Michael S. Yamashita/Corbis; p. 33 © George Hall/Corbis; p. 34 © Chris Rainier/Corbis; p. 36 © Corbis; p. 39 © Chris Rainier/Corbis; p. 41 © Jim Sugar Photography/Corbis; p. 43 © Aero Graphics, Inc./Corbis.

Visit Children's Press on the Internet at:
http://publishing.grolier.com

Library of Congress Cataloging-in-Publication Data

Kennedy, Robert C.
  Life in the Marines / by Robert C. Kennedy.
    p. cm. – (On duty)
  Includes bibliographical references and index.
  Summary: Presents a brief history of the United States Marine Corps, explains how to enter the Corps and what types of jobs and training are available, and gives a detailed description of the twelve weeks of boot camp.
  ISBN 0-516-23348-3 (lib. bdg.) – ISBN 0-516-23548-6 (pbk.)
    1. United States. Marine Corps—Vocational guidance—Juvenile literature.
    [1. United
  States Marine Corps—Vocational guidance. 2. Vocational guidance.] I. Title. II. Series.

VE23.K46 2000
359.9'6'0973—dc21
                                                00-024035

CONTENTS

Introduction

The United States Marine Corps is one of the most respected of all military forces. The corps was created in 1775 at Tun Tavern in Philadelphia, Pennsylvania. The American colonies were preparing to fight the American Revolutionary War (1775–1783). The corps was later formally commissioned (chosen) by the Second Continental Congress.

Marines fought heroically in several Revolutionary battles. Their first amphibious assault (attack from the water) was in March 1776. In that attack, the Marines captured Fort Montagu and Fort Nassau on New Province Island, in the Bahamas. They surprised the forts by attacking from the sea. They landed men on the shore and overcame the British soldiers.

Marines wear ID tags known as "dog tags" around their necks.

Congress dismissed the corps members in 1783. The corps was brought back fifteen years later. The Marines have been a fighting force for the United States ever since. Today, marines are trained to be some of the best and smartest soldiers in the world.

HOW TO GET
THERE FROM HERE

WHO THEY ARE

The Marines are a separate military force within the U.S. Department of the Navy. The word marine means of or relating to the sea.

The U.S. Marine Corps is a huge organization. Today there are more than 172,000 men and women serving in the Marines. Marines work as typists, chefs, auto mechanics, or undercover military police. Some marines fight wars on the battlefront. Others support the fighting marines with work done far from enemy lines. What they all have in common is that they are members of the Marine Corps.

People who join the Marines are looking for a sense of honor, courage and commitment. These values are learned in just three months of Marine Corp boot camp. They give young

Marines sometimes use helicopters to drop into enemy areas.

men and women the pride and confidence that comes with fighting for one's country.

WHAT THEY DO

The Marine Corps's mission is to conduct sea and land operations. As this is written, marines are enforcing a 1991 treaty (agreement) signed by Iraq and the United Nations (UN). This treaty limits the amount of oil that Iraq can sell. Marines are stationed in the Persian Gulf to search oil tankers. They test samples of the oil the tanker carries. The test tells from where the oil came. Marines will do this until Iraq begins following the treaty. If the oil is from Iraq, the tanker may be seized.

Marines are also the U.S. president's guard of honor. Honor guards stand guard during ceremonies in which the president participates. Honor guards can be seen in photos or televised news stories. They lead the president into a room or onto a stage. Often they stand inside the doors of a room the president enters.

Barbed wire is just one way marines keep enemies out of an area.

Marines are responsible for the president's short helicopter trips. They pilot the helicopter that takes the president to Camp David or to the airport to board Air Force One.

Sometimes marines serve on Navy ships. When a ship is at sea or in port, the security of secret papers, equipment, and crew members are part of a marine's duties.

The Marine security guard (MSG) battalion protects American embassies and consulates in other countries. Marines handle the security of people, secret papers, and equipment inside these buildings.

ENTERING THE CORPS AS AN OFFICER

To join the Marines, officer recruits must be between twenty and twenty-eight years old. Recruits take one of the following routes to earn a reserve (temporary) or regular (permanent) appointment as a commissioned officer:

Naval Reserve Officers' Training Corps (NROTC)

The armed forces pay tuition and other benefits worth up to $70,000 for four years of service. High school graduates can get four-year scholarships. Graduates of NROTC receive commissions as reserve officers.

Platoon Leaders Class (PLC)

All first-year college students, sophomores, or juniors may train only during the summer months. After one summer at Officer Candidate School in Quantico, Virginia, they receive $150 per month in financial aid. Graduates get a reserve commission.

Some Marines are trained for special mountain duty.

Officer Candidate Class (OCC)

College seniors and graduates may take a post-graduate training course of ten weeks and get a reserve commission.

U.S. Naval Academy

High school graduates may get a congressional appointment to the academy at Annapolis, Maryland. A graduate of the academy earns a Bachelor of Science degree and a regular commission.

ENTERING THE CORPS AS AN ENLISTED PERSON

More than 95 percent of people who join the Marines come in as enlisted soldiers. They must be between seventeen and twenty-eight years of age. They choose jobs from more than three hundred military occupation specialties (MOS). Some of these jobs include weather specialists, intelligence (information) officers, and firefighters. The Marines also employs construction workers, tank officers, and accountants. The Marine Corps is like a community. Every community needs many different people to make it successful. MOS training is taken after completing boot camp and advanced combat training.

New recruits are trained in San Diego, California, or at Parris Island, South Carolina. All have similar experiences to talk about later. However, this book refers only to the East Coast training centers.

Airborne assaults are a quick way to get marines into an area.

HOW MARINES ARE ORGANIZED

The U.S. Department of Defense commands all military forces. They are the Department of the Army, the Department of the Air Force and the Department of the Navy. The Navy has a special military force under its direction: The U.S. Marine Corps. It's commanded by a four-star general.

The Marine Corps has three infantry divisions and three air wings. Infantry are foot soldiers. Air wings use aircraft to fight.

MARINE EXPEDITIONARY FORCE (MEF)

The Marine expeditionary force (MEF) is the main combat organization of the U.S. Marine Corps. It handles large military operations. The Gulf War (1991) is an example of the type of operation that the MEF operates. The MEF is commanded by a three-star lieutenant general.

THE MARINE AIR-GROUND TASK FORCE (MAGTF)

Marine divisions (groups of fighters) are organized into a larger Marine air-ground task force (MAGTF). A MAGTF can quickly reach a trouble spot. The MAGTF stays at sea, but close to shore. This tells the people causing trouble that they had better think twice before attacking.

THE MARINE EXPEDITIONARY UNIT (MEU)

The Marine expeditionary unit (MEU) is built around three forces—an infantry battalion, an

Marines are used to traveling by water.

aircraft squadron (group), and a service support group. Altogether, the MEU has more than two thousand marines. The MEU carries out small operations for U.S. Naval forces. When an MEU leaves its home station, it must be special operations capable (SOC). Special operations may include the use of SEAL (SEa Air and Land) teams. A SEAL team is trained and equipped to secretly slip into enemy areas. The team may include both sailors and marines. It can go into a mission by ship, hovercraft, submarine, helicopter, parachute, or by swimming.

THE REGIMENTAL RESERVE

The Marines can put a combat force of fifteen thousand men into any part of the world with two weeks' notice. Everything they need to do the job is stored on bases in different parts of the world:

- A U.S. Marine base in Norway
- Maritime prepositioning ships (MPS) in the Mediterranean Sea
- Guam, a U.S. territory in the western part of the Pacific Ocean
- Diego Garcia, an island in the Indian Ocean

WHERE DO YOU FIT?

If you don't go to an MOS school after boot camp, you'll start out in the infantry. Advanced infantry training after boot camp prepares you for combat. After advanced infantry training, you are ready to be called to go to war.

You'll be in a squad of twelve to fifteen marines. A squad is part of a larger group, called a battalion. A battalion is the largest part of the MEU.

There is not always a war going on in the world that involves the Marines. However, when war breaks out, the Marines are ready to fight for peace. In the meantime, marines are constantly training. Training keeps marines ready. Training helps them to succeed on the battlefield.

Marine training is a tough test of a recruit's
physical and mental abilities.

17

MAKING MEN AND WOMEN MARINES

Marine training begins the very first day at boot camp. A drill instructor (DI) is a recruit's teacher and mentor (someone to look up to). DIs are highly trained sergeants who are expert teachers. They have proven themselves to be superior marines. Therefore, they have been asked to train new recruits. Drill instructors understand what recruits must go through to become marines. They know how far to push their recruits. They also help recruits to make it through basic training.

The training program lasts twelve weeks. One of the Marines's boot camp training facilities is at Parris Island, South Carolina. The following is what happens during the twelve-week boot camp and advanced training courses.

Marines often help each other during training.

PROCESSING

Recruits spend their first three days in receiving. During these three days, recruits quickly learn what Marine life will be like.

Men and women get a standard haircut. Men have their heads shaved. Women have their hair cut short. Recruits are fitted for and issued uniforms and footwear. They are given toiletries and some writing supplies. Recruits receive medical and dental examinations. Recruits meet their senior DI. Finally, recruits take an initial strength test. This test measures each recruit's incoming ability. From this point, a recruit's physical fitness is measured against that first test. Recruits will have to improve their physical fitness to pass boot camp.

FORMING

Recruits are formed into training companies, platoons, and squads. During this three-to-five-day period, they learn to make beds, clean

Wearing the same kinds of clothes and training together builds unity in Marine troops.

latrines (toilets), and march in formation. They also learn how to wear uniforms, clean weapons, shine shoes, and clean gear. This training allows recruits to adjust to military life. It also gives them a chance to make friends. Making friends is helpful to every recruit. By the time boot camp is over, they will have helped friends and gotten help from others.

WEEKS ONE THROUGH FOUR

Recruits learn how to march. Marching teaches discipline, pride, and company unity. Recruits also learn general military subjects. These include both Marine and military history, insignia (badge and rank recognition), and military courtesy (acting like a proper marine).

Physical training (PT) is important to marines. Every marine must be able to push his or her body and mind to its limits. Therefore, physical training is increased as the days and weeks progress. Recruits do sit-ups, push-ups, and chin-ups. They increase how many they can do each day. Running is part of PT. Running helps to build physical endurance.

Obstacle courses and three-, five- or ten-mile marches build endurance. In the obstacle course, recruits must run over, crawl under, and walk across all types of obstacles. They have to complete the course in a certain amount of time.

Drill instructors give talks after a demanding program of PT or a long march. The talks help recruits to focus. They are useful to recruits who feel that they have reached their physical and mental limit. Recruits call this limit the "wall." Recruits who've hit the wall feel that they are unable to go further. This is where teamwork comes in. Friends help each other make it past these tough parts of basic training.

Close combat training teaches survival tactics. During this training, recruits use pugil sticks to learn bayonet fighting. Pugil sticks are six-foot-long sticks with padded knobs at each end. Two recruits fight against each other to learn how to hit an enemy and defend against

Training helps recruits learn what life is like as a marine.

being hit. Recruits learn how to survive fighting with a bayonet or with no weapon at all.

The confidence course is eleven different bodybuilding challenges. Monkey bars, jumps, hurdles, walls, and rope climbs are a few examples. Completing this course quickly builds a recruit's confidence in him- or herself.

The physical training and teamwork learned in weeks one through four prepare recruits for the next ten weeks. Weeks five through fourteen are demanding for recruits.

WEEK FIVE

Combat water survival teaches recruits to move through water at many depths. They learn to cross streams. They learn how to swim in deep water while wearing clothes and boots. Recruits are tested after the training. Those who want to be SEALs take a more difficult test. They are tested wearing full combat gear, with rifle, helmet, flak jacket and pack.

The confidence course tests recruits' ability to move quickly over obstacles.

WEEK SIX

Basic warrior training puts recruits into field living conditions. Most field training occurs after recruit training. Basic warrior training is an introduction to what a marine does during battle. Recruits set up tents and learn about field cleanliness and camouflage. They rappel (slide down by rope) from a tower.

Recruits also practice tear gas attacks. This training teaches recruits to quickly put on gas masks while tear gas is released around them. They must train to fight while wearing gas masks. All recruits must pass the gas chamber test. Here, a group of six or ten recruits are sent into a chamber while wearing their gas masks. Gas is released in the chamber. The recruits learn how to breathe through their masks. Then they must take off their masks and walk out of the chamber.

WEEKS SEVEN AND EIGHT

These are snap-in weeks. During these two weeks the four shooting positions are taught: standing, kneeling, sitting, and prone (lying on the ground). A primary marksmanship instructor demonstrates how to fire the M16A2 rifle. He teaches recruits how to adjust the sights. During week seven, recruits use a model gun against a video display. During week eight, they

Recruits must successfully learn how to use tear gas masks.

fire a real rifle on ranges. The range has targets set at distances of 100 yards and further. On Friday of week eight, recruits are tested. They must shoot accurately to qualify to use their weapon.

WEEK NINE

This is Team Week. There are no training days! Recruits form teams and compete in relay races and tugs-of-war. Team week builds unit teamwork while having fun.

WEEK TEN

This week teaches A-line training. Recruits are taught to fire their weapons at multiple targets from one position. Recruits also must learn how to shoot accurately while wearing a gas mask.

WEEK ELEVEN

Transformation week is the last week of recruit training. It's called The Crucible. This is the

The Crucible is a 54-hour test that puts recruits through battle conditions to see how they perform.

final test of recruits as individuals and as a team. The Crucible includes going with only 4 hours of sleep in 54 hours. This test is taken in the field, under whatever weather conditions are present. It requires teamwork to solve a series of problems while overcoming obstacles and helping each other to make it.

Upon successful completion of The Crucible, the drill instructor presents each recruit with a Marine badge: the Eagle, Globe, and Anchor. From that moment on, the trainee is never again called a recruit. The recruit has become a member of the U.S. Marine Corps!

WEEK TWELVE

Transition week is the last week trainees spend on Parris Island. The new marines are expected to take responsibility for themselves. They must act like marines. They must show their dedication to duty, honor, and courage.

Family day and graduation are the last two days at boot camp. A formal ceremony and parade commemorate this memorable event in a marine's life. Family members are invited to the base. They sit in the stands and watch as Marine units march onto the parade grounds in full dress uniform. A marine's uniform may show medals for marksmanship or leadership. The graduation ceremony presents recruits with the congratulations from drill instructors, commanding officers, and family members.

After a ten-day leave (vacation), all the marines go to Camp Lejune, North Carolina. Infantry marines go to the Infantry Training Battalion, School of Infantry, for MOS training.

Graduation day is a time for celebration.
Recruits have become members of the U.S. Marine Corps.

Noninfantry marines are assigned to the Marine Combat Training (MCT) Battalion, School of Infantry. The difference between these two training courses is the level of training that is given. The infantry marine groups learn much more about fighting in the field. Noninfantry training teaches marines how to support the infantry. This support includes all of those everyday jobs that one might find in the civilian world.

MARINES ON DUTY

Day-to-day Marine life is centered around training. Marines must train to keep up their fighting skills. Marines are not always fighting in wars. However, marines are always stationed throughout the world. The jobs that marines perform around the world serve many different purposes.

SECRET ENTRANCE INTO ENEMY AREAS

One important task of the Marines is to get soldiers into an area without being detected. Another part of this operation is to keep their destination a secret. Marines use helicopters, boats, and submarines to keep their movements undetected.

Helicopters are a swift way of getting marines into and out of an area.

QUICK HUMANITARIAN RESPONSE

The Marines are not just a fighting force. The Marines help when disaster strikes. When disasters such as floods, earthquakes, tornadoes, and hurricanes strike, marines transport food, clothing, and shelter to the affected areas. Such disasters also damage or destroy homes and other buildings. Marines help clean up the wreckage.

SHOWING THEIR FORCE

Some nations still attack other nations. When this happens, the nation that is attacked will usually ask for help. The United States is asked for help many times each year. Often it sends Marine forces to an area to show that the United States will fight unless the attacking nation stops its war. At such times, Marine forces stay just outside an area, often on ships off the shore of the warring nation. Such a show of force can make the warring nation back down.

HELP COUNTRIES BATTLE WARRING NATIONS

When warring nations do not back down, it is the job of the Marines to fight. When they are called to move in and fight, they quickly organize. Such small invasions often help to stop armed conflict between warring countries. The attacking nation sees the Marines as a danger

Marines often serve as peacekeepers in nations
where people are fighting each other.

35

to its plans. It backs off from the fight. Other times, Marine fighting forces must stay longer. This situation happens when an attacking nation doesn't back off from its fight. Then Marine forces will use more firepower, such as tanks and jet fighters.

SEND IN REINFORCEMENTS

During war, not all of a country's soldiers are sent into battle at once. Many are kept behind the lines, or even at home. They are kept in reserve. They may go to battle, or they may just train for the possibility.

Marines are one such battle force. They hold back many soldiers from every battle. These soldiers continue to train. They may be sent to this battle, or they may be sent to another battle.

STAY AFTER THE BATTLE IS OVER

Quick wars don't happen very often. Most of the time wars take weeks, months, or even years. Wars cause a lot of destruction. Homes are wrecked. Entire cities can be destroyed. Such damage sends people running away. Once the war is over, those people must return to their homes.

Large Marine forces are taken to an area by transport plane.

37

Marine forces often stay after a battle is done. They stay to help people begin their lives again. Marines help to clean up damaged towns. They help to rebuild roads, bridges, and buildings. Marine forces also help peaceful local and national governments to begin working again.

LEAVE ONCE PEACE IS RESTORED

After a nation's people and government are restored to peace, marines go home. Their job is finished, so they are no longer needed. Marines pack up their gear and begin to leave the area. Sometimes leaving an area takes time. When this happens, marines group together and live in tents or special housing until they can leave.

Marines performing humanitarian aid like to make friends with local people.

LOOKING AHEAD

There always will be changes in the way marines train, deploy, and fight. This will happen because of the places and types of battles they will have to fight. Many future battles around the world will happen in cities. Marines must be ready and trained to fight in such places.

The role of women in key command positions will grow in the service support groups and air wings. Already, 93 percent of all occupational fields and 62 percent of all jobs are open to female marines. They still cannot serve in the infantry, armor, or artillery. These are combat fighting units. However, women do fly helicopters and jets in the Marines. As our civilian work force becomes less aware of gender, the Marine Corps will follow suit.

THE FUTURE OF COMBAT

As you read this, naval architects probably are hunched over blueprints for a new type of

Marine units are on the watch for trouble all over the world.

aircraft carrier. These carriers might be called MEU attack transports (MEUAT). The old, huge aircraft carriers still will handle the Navy jets and rescue helicopters. But the MEUAT will handle the vertical/short takeoff and landing (V/STOL) aircraft (Harrier AV-8B II) and other helicopters and hovercraft (propeller-powered boats). The MEU attack transports will be able to quickly send out fighting forces.

Because large fleet carriers must stay in deep waters, the MEUAT could move into shallow harbors and bays. That would put it closer to the battle area and save precious time and fuel for all vehicles used by the MEU.

The Harrier AV-8B II

One attack aircraft is ready for the MEUAT. It's the AV-8B Harrier II. This jet fighter can lift off like a helicopter, and then fly forward under jet power. Such a plane doesn't need a runway. It can land and take off from a jungle clearing or

The Harrier jet fighter is a perfect plane for the Marines. It doesn't need a runway to take off and land.

a city street. Such a plane is an important weapon for the Marines.

EYES ON THE ROAD AND THE WATER

Whatever future battles lay before the Marines, they will be ready to fight. Their organization and training helps them daily to deal with the changing world. No marine wants to go to war. However, when the call to battle is given, the Marines are capable of battlefield glory.

New Words

amphibious of or from the sea, as in an amphibious landing or amphibious assault

battalion military unit, made up of three or more companies

company military unit, made up of three or more platoons

corps military unit, usually made up of three or more infantry divisions

division military unit, usually made up of three or more brigades or regiments

drill instructor (DI) training instructor, usually an experienced sergeant

infantry ground troops or foot soldiers

mission assigned task to complete

pugil stick long wooden pole with padded ends used in bayonet training

rappel to make a controlled drop, by rope, from a helicopter, cliff, or building

SEAL Navy SEa, Air, and Land unit, for special operations and secret missions

For Further Reading

Cureton, Charles H. *The United States Marine Corps: From 1775 to Modern Day*. Broomall, PA: Chelsea House Publishers, 1999.

Green, Michael. *The United States Marine Corps*. Danbury. CT: Children's Press, 1998.

Green, Michael. *The United States Navy*. Danbury, CT, Children's Press, 1998.

Hole, Dorothy. *The Marines and You*. Parsippany, NJ: Silver Burdett Press, 1993.

Rummel, Jack. *The U.S. Marine Corps*. Broomall, PA: Chelsea House Publishers, 1990.

Sweetman, Jack. American Naval History: *An Illustrated Chronology of the U.S. Navy and Marine Corps*, 1775-Present. Annapolis, MD: Naval Institute Press, 1991.

Resources

MarineLINK

www.usmc.mil

This site offers news and information about the Marine Corps, including details of recent operations and recent exercises. It also describes the history and traditions of the Marine Corps.

National Headquarters of the Marine Corps League

P.O. Box 3070

Merrifield, VA 22116

(800) 625-1775

www.mcleague.org

The Marine Corps League is committed to "preserving the traditions and promoting the interests of the United States Marine Corps."

U.S. Army Homepage

www.army.mil

This is the official site of the U. S. Army. It includes current news, recruiting information, and links to other branches of the Army.

Index

Index

About the Author

Robert C. Kennedy entered the U.S. Army at age seventeen and attended various specialized schools. He served with a military intelligence detachment during the Korean War and with a special operations detachment during the Vietnam War, in 1967. He ended his career as an instructor for the Military Intelligence Officer Advanced Course, which he helped to develop, in 1968.